RADICAL BUSINESS

RADICAL
BUSINESS
FROM OWNERSHIP TO STEWARDSHIP

GARY RINGGER
Forward by Rod Brenneman

Radical Business
From Ownership to Stewardship
Gary Ringger

Copyright © 2018 by Gary Ringger

ISBN: 978-1-5323-8635-0

Printed in China

TABLE OF CONTENTS

FOREWORD

I was both honored and humbled when Gary asked me to write the foreword for this book. Gary shares example after example of how God has provided for him in his personal and business life. God has orchestrated so many things in Gary's life, as He does for all of us, and our connecting and becoming friends was no different.

We had been briefly introduced through a common business interest but had never had a conversation; we didn't know each other at all. But then, one day we were both in a small regional airport at the exact same time (clearly a God thing) and Gary was several people behind me in the security line. I hear this voice from behind me calling out my name and the rest is history. We spent a little time in the airport getting to know each other and then he drove from Illinois to Kansas City to meet with me and share what he was doing at Lifesong.

Our friendship developed over several years. I was the CEO for two different companies and Gary continued to "prod" me to get more involved with him in ministry. As I transitioned from my CEO role, I began to look at what the next chapter of my life would involve. More importantly, how could my wife and I impact the Kingdom with the resources God had entrusted to us? Gary's advice of becoming "focused and involved" resonated with me. This led to many telephone conversations, coffee shop meetings, and yes, spreadsheet reviews to discuss how we might use our common interest of business as an engine for Kingdom purposes, beyond what either of us could ever ask or imagine.

I believe this book will challenge you, push you, encourage you and excite you to take a radical look at how you might be called to impact the Kingdom. Through Gary's story, and his passion to do the extraordinary things, I believe you will start to look at your life's work with a different perspective. Gary and I have kicked around so many ideas, some of which were good and others that were not so good, and through it all God has opened and closed many doors. But the most amazing thing has been how God has prompted me to look at business in a different way... a *radical* way. Certainly, Gary has been a remarkable brother and encourager God used for that purpose.

My prayer is that God will do the same for you as you read this book.

ROD BRENNEMAN
Former CEO of Butterball

LIVING THE ADVENTURE[1]

Author unknown

*When I met Christ, it seemed as though life was rather like
a bike ride. But it was a tandem bike, and I noticed that
Christ was in the back helping me pedal.*

*I don't know just when it was that He suggested
we change places, but life has not been the same
since. When I had control, I knew the way. It was rather
boring and predictable... It was the shortest distance
between two points.*

*But when He took the lead, He knew delightful
long cuts up mountains and through rocky places
at breakneck speeds; it was all I could do to hang on!
Even though it looked like madness, He said, "Pedal!"*

I worried and was anxious and asked, "Where are you taking me?" He laughed and didn't answer, and I started to learn to trust. I forgot my boring life and entered into the adventure. And when I'd say, " I'm scared!" He'd lean back and touch my hand.

He took me to people with gifts that I needed, gifts of healing, acceptance, and joy. They gave me gifts to take on my journey, my Lord's and mine. And we were off again.

He said, "Give the gifts away; they're extra baggage, too much weight." So I did, to the people we met, and I found that in giving I received.

I did not trust Him, at first, in control of my life. I thought He'd wreck it; but he knows bike secrets, knows how to make it bend to make sharp corners, knows how to jump to clear high rocks, knows how to fly to shorten scary passages.

And I am learning to shut up and pedal in the strangest
places, and I'm beginning to enjoy the view,
and the cool breeze on my face, with my delightful
constant companion, Jesus Christ.

And when I'm sure I can't do anymore,
He just smiles and says... "Pedal."

PART 1
THE CONTRACT

CHAPTER 1
BROKEN

I wake up with a start. I've broken out in a cold sweat and my heart is beating in my head like a manic drummer. Fear and confusion muddle my mind as I gaze at the clock: 1:07 AM. I'm trying to figure out what's happening to me as I face another sleepless night. By nature, I'm easy-going and usually roll with the punches. But not now. Not tonight. Tonight, I'm filled with fear and anxiety. I'm realizing how fine the line is between emotional health and emotional chaos, and I know that my struggle to succeed is at the heart of it.

I wasn't a very serious college student. My original major was Business Administration, but that required 54 credit hours for a degree, so when I found out a degree in Economics only required 36 hours, I made the switch to Econ. That would give me more time to take music theory and group piano classes taught by a professor who played a mean jazz piano.

When I graduated from college, I had no idea what I wanted to do with the rest of my life. I remember telling my dad (after receiving a college degree he had paid for) I wanted to spend the next year practicing piano and working on my music. A worried look clouded his eyes and he told me he had a better idea. A few weeks later I started working for him in our family feed business. If things went well, I could run the business someday. This was a promising opportunity.

My first job with Ringger Feeds was spent in the production room mixing and bagging pig feed. It was a dirty, dusty job. I remember when a friend from high school stopped by. I was covered in green alfalfa meal. He looked me over and said "Gary, why are you doing this when you have a college degree?"

But, my dad had a plan. He thought I should learn the business from the ground up. In time, he started sending me out on customer sales calls. I soon found I enjoyed the challenge and the interaction with customers and prospects. My "aha moment" came after I met a swine nutritionist. I learned from him that if we manufactured our feed from scratch, instead of buying a blend, our product cost dropped significantly. We could lower our price to our customers and double our margin at the same time. It was magic! It was the moment when I fell in love with business and knew what I wanted to do with the rest of my life.

It didn't take long before I was actively managing the company. And though titles didn't mean much in our small family business, I became vice president. With margins doubled and more revenue coming in, I began to hire salesmen and develop a professional team. As I took on more responsibility, Dad spent less time in the business. He was involved in our church as a lay pastor, which was where his passion and energy were. So, I decided it was appropriate that I

receive a title promotion to increase my credibility. I called
Dad at home one afternoon and woke him from a nap.

"Hey Dad, I want to give you a promotion."

"That sounds good," He replied groggily, "What kind of
a promotion?"

"You should be the big CEO – how does that sound?"

"That sounds good!'

"Great," I responded, "Because I want to be the president!"

"That sounds good too!" He laughed. And just like that, I
promoted myself to president of Ringger Feeds.

As president, my responsibility was to chart the future
course of the company and I began to see myself as quite
the visionary. My brother Earl, who was our production
manager, also recognized this trait in me. At one point
he said,

"Gary, you come up with all these good ideas, but you expect us to implement them and that takes time. So here is my idea. While we (our executive team) work out your latest plan, we're going to blindfold and gag you and put you in a corner and you can think up your next idea. When we finish setting up your last idea, we will un-blindfold and un-gag you. Then you can tell us your new idea, and we will do it all over again!"

Starting a food company was one of my new ideas. Through the course of business, I had the opportunity to visit a Kraft Foods manufacturing plant. I remember walking from room to room observing a different process in each one. I thought, "Wow, I've never seen a plant like this in the feed industry!" The size and scope hit me as I realized the potential in the food industry. After all, people would always need food to eat. I decided that someday I was going to manufacture food for human consumption.

I started dreaming, asking questions and talking to business contacts and anyone else connected to the food industry. I met a food scientist, Susan, who had her own dream. Susan was working with a large sugar company that manufactured the powdered white sugar used to coat donuts. Her idea was to make a variety of different flavors of donut coatings and market them to supermarkets across the United States, but she needed someone to mix and bag her product. Since I had experience mixing and bagging feed, it made sense that I would mix coatings for Susan. This would be a slam dunk!

So, in the summer of 1986, we bought a little machine shed at the west end of our small town of Gridley, Illinois, population 1200, and started Ringger Foods. Although I knew little about the food industry, the visit to the Kraft plant had ignited something within me. There was so much opportunity. The food market is HUGE and I believed we could capitalize on manufacturing food products. I told my wife, Marla, "My goal is to get rich, retire when I'm 40 and we will live the American Dream!"

It didn't take long for reality to set in. I quickly learned that starting a new business was much harder than growing an existing one. Ringger Foods began losing money immediately and the responsibility of making "people food" instead of "pig food" began to wear on me in a big way.

I knew almost nothing about food safety, and the more I learned about how little I knew, the more my anxiety grew.

For several months, night after night, I would wake up in the wee hours of the morning in a cold sweat, my heart racing. I would lie awake with dark thoughts, worrying we were going to kill someone with bacteria tainted donut coatings. As this continued, I became sleep deprived and overwhelmed. Vince Lombardi once said, "Fatigue makes cowards of us all." I felt the truth of this; it was making a coward of me. As depression and desperation set in, the American dream I had been so excited about faded into meaninglessness. I wanted my life back. I wanted to quit. Ringger Feeds was doing well. Our family had all we needed. Ringger Foods was failing and I wanted to shut it down.

Thankfully, God met me in my desperation and need. Psalm 34:18 says, *"The LORD is close to the brokenhearted; he rescues those whose spirits are crushed."* I was broken before God and as I pleaded and prayed about what to do next, I felt the Holy Spirit say, "Don't quit. Change your paradigm." As I prayerfully considered what that meant, I slowly began to have renewed hope and excitement for the future of Ringger Foods. An idea began to grow in my mind. I believed this idea was inspired by God. The idea was to make a written contract with God that said,

"If Ringger Foods ever becomes successful and we sell it, we will pay our investment back with interest; but the remaining balance will be used for Kingdom purposes."

I wrote out this simple contract on a piece of notebook paper and showed it to Marla and Dad. They both knew how tired and depressed I had become and saw how this could help me get on with my life, so they readily agreed. This new direction was exciting for all of us. Because Ringger Foods had no value, the contract did not feel like a sacrifice, but, it held the promise of a partnership with God, and that was exciting.

Dad and I signed the contract.

Of course, the business did not turn around all at once. In fact, the donut coating business never became successful so we ultimately had to explore other opportunities, but a weight had been lifted and I could sleep again at night. The business was no longer "mine," and in the years that followed I would occasionally say, "Dad, this is God's business." Based on the red ink the business was accumulating, he would smile and say, "I'm not sure God wants this business." Regardless, the contract had changed my mindset, allowing me to learn many lessons in my partnership with Him.

———

LESSONS LEARNED FROM THE FATHER

1. **Make yourself accountable.** I wrote out the contract on a piece of paper and Dad and I signed it. This kept us accountable. Years later, when Ringger Foods was sold, my dear dad, who had not gone through the sleepless nights and depression, came to me and said, "Gary you can do whatever you want with your half but I would like to divide my half between you and your brother and sister".

My dad had forgotten about the contract.

If we had not written it down, I might have, too. Not only that, but I am sure we would have wondered what that commitment we made 15 years before really meant. I remember pulling out the contract and showing it to Dad. He saw his signature and being a man of integrity, immediately endorsed it. To him, every commitment must be honored, especially those made with God. Writing the contract and physically signing it kept us accountable to the promise we had made.

2. **Be a Steward.** The contract gave me a steward mindset versus an owner mindset. A steward is someone who manages or looks after another person's property. One advantage of being a steward is it takes away the pride of ownership. In addition, when you are the owner, human nature tends to make you prone to abuse power. But, when God is the owner and you're working for Him, you understand your role is to manage the business in the way He would want. How you treat employees, customers, and venders is a direct result of the owner's wishes.

3. **Realize it's all His.** The contract lessened the risk of putting money before God. When Jesus challenged the rich

young ruler to sell what he had and give it all to the poor, he walked away sorrowfully because he couldn't release his wealth to the Lord. Jesus emphasized the danger of money so much that the apostles asked, *"How, then, can a rich man be saved?"* To which Jesus answered, *"All things are possible with God."* Making the contract before the business was successful took away this temptation. I believe if the business had already been successful, I wouldn't have made the contract, and I would have missed out on some of my life's richest blessings.

4. **Have a purpose bigger than yourself.** The contract gave me a purpose bigger than myself. It gave me the courage and energy to keep pressing forward. Prior to the contract, my goal was to retire at 40 so I could spend time relaxing, playing music and tennis. Now that I am older, I love to get away and relax, but I soon get restless. I am eager to get back to work, because work for me means making a difference in God's Kingdom.

Bill Bright, founder of Campus Crusade for Christ, was interviewed shortly before he passed away by Dennis Rainey, founder of Family Life. Dennis said, "Bill you're still highly motivated, even at 81 years of age. You're on oxygen 24 hours a day and your lungs are only working at about 40% of capacity. What gets you out of bed?"

"Well my love for Jesus." Bill quickly responded.

He then went on to enthusiastically describe the project he was currently working on and how God was using him during his last days on earth.

That's how I want to live my last days - working for Jesus. And because I'm involved in a purpose bigger than myself, I believe I will.

THINGS TO CONSIDER

1. Prayerfully consider your business goals and then ask yourself. Am I a steward or an owner?
2. Listen to Bill Bright's interview on the following link: *www.radicalbusiness.co/resources* I listen to it periodically and it always blesses me.
3. Is there a business commitment you need to write down so you won't forget it later?

PART 2

UNEXPECTED BLESSINGS

CHAPTER 2
INTIMATE PRAYER

I walk out to the deck and ease into the hot tub.

Snowflakes are falling and it is beautiful! Automatically,

I begin to recite,

"Our Father which art in heaven, Hallowed be thy name..."

The contract gave me a new outlook but it did not change my circumstances overnight. I was still struggling with depression and a failing business. I'm a creative person and that seemed to compound my depression. It was hard for me to make decisions because I would see all kinds of options. Based on my overwhelmed and defeated state of mind, I couldn't decide what option to take. I didn't want to make any more mistakes, and my mind was spinning, like tires on ice, unable to get any positive traction or direction.

Each morning, I would wake up feeling overwhelmed. How could I get out of this daily pattern? God had an answer for me. He used a book on prayer and my hot tub to turn this struggle into a blessing.

The book was a compilation of essays written by early Christians. These were men from the early church; some of the first believers who lived after Christ's ascension into heaven, and many (if not all) were martyred for their faith. They were serious about their walk with Christ and serious about prayer, and as I read their writings, I noticed they viewed the Lord's Prayer much more literally than I did.

The Lord's Prayer was how they prayed!

I had memorized this prayer as a kid but never considered it like these men did. Influenced by their writings, I determined to be more literal in my interpretation of how Christ taught us to pray. I wanted to pray more like these saints of old.

I also made three types of prayer lists: one for my family, one for others, and one for ministry. I seldom used prayer lists in the past, but now it became a daily practice.

Our hot tub was where I met God in prayer. I had heard that to encourage meditation, worship, and prayer time, you should have a special place in nature (or elsewhere) that you enjoy – a place where you would like to spend time conversing with your Father and meditating on His goodness and power. Our hot tub sat on the deck outside our bedroom. It was private, peaceful and beautiful. Each morning, when I would wake up feeling overwhelmed, I would stumble out of bed, head to the hot tub and begin my daily prayer. There, God would renew my mind so that by the time I finished meditating on the Lord's Prayer, I was ready to face the day. My prayers would go something like this:

Our Father which art in heaven, Hallowed be thy name.
I would reflect on my Father's attributes; an all-powerful, loving and sovereign God who wants what's best for me. Why should I worry when He is in control?

Thy Kingdom come, thy will be done on earth as it is in heaven. I would think about how I want His will to be done and not my will, because I trust Him more than I trust myself.

Give us today our daily bread. I would go through my prayer lists for family, others and ministry. My ministry list focused on Ringger Foods. I would lay out all my questions to my Father each day. How should I handle this situation? There is an opportunity to work with this broker, to manufacture this product, to invest in this equipment. What should I do? And then I would relax and wait for Him to answer.

Forgive us our debts as we forgive our debtors. I seldom struggled with hurt feelings, but if I did, my Father would bring the person I was struggling with to mind and I would ask for grace to forgive and turn those feelings over to Him.

Lead us not into temptation but deliver us from evil. I would ask God to keep me out of trouble.

For Thine is the Kingdom and the power and the glory forever amen! I would pray, "God you are Awesome! Thank you for being my Father!"

Prior to the contract, my prayer life was a discipline. I believed in the power of prayer and I knew it was for my benefit, but it was something I had to make sure I spent time doing each day. After the contract, my prayer time went from being a discipline to being a necessity. I needed His guidance to go out and face the day. If I missed time alone with the Father, I felt unarmed and unprepared for the challenges I would face.

Before the contract, my prayers were rigid and formal. If my mind wandered during my prayer, I would feel guilty, like I was being disrespectful to Jesus. Now I just enjoyed the quiet time with Him, sometimes praying and sometimes falling asleep. If I fell asleep, it was ok. I didn't feel any guilt. It was like sitting by the pool in Florida with Marla, enjoying laid-back conversation or sleeping on a chaise lounge, simply happy to be with her, basking in the warmth of the sun.

Prayer time had become my favorite part of the day!

The more I started my day in fellowship with the Lord, the easier it was for me to make decisions. Solutions to problems that were bugging me would come to my mind, often during "tub time." I would bring questions and concerns to the Father daily and then I would seek out and listen to counsel from wise and godly men. If I had peace about a decision, I would accept it in faith and act. If I was bathing (pun intended) the decision in prayer, I had confidence my Father would let me know if I should move forward or not. Colossians 3:17 (LB) says, *"Let the peace of God tell you what to do."* Prayer time allowed me to live this verse in a new and real way.

I began to experience God's divine intervention in tangible ways, more than I ever had before. I remember when, based on the poor financial performance of Ringger Foods, Dad, Steph Baner (our Ringger Feeds/Ringger Foods CFO), and I decided to put out a fleece before God.

We met off site and talked about how Ringger Foods' red ink was starting to affect the health of Ringger Feeds. We wrote down a specific date, asking God to guide us. Our "fleece" stated that if Ringger Foods was not a profitable business by that date, we would shut it down.

Several weeks later, Nutri-Sweet contacted us after seeing a small classified ad we had placed in a food magazine. Nutri-Sweet was building a new plant and needed someone to blend Equal for them in the interim. At their current plant, they were using a Littleford blender and because our ad mentioned we had one, we were an attractive option for them. We began negotiations and within the "fleece date parameter" they awarded us a lucrative contract. Their purchasing agent commented that she had a "gut feeling" about us. We praised God for giving her what we believed was the Holy Spirit's nudge. The Nutri-Sweet contract was huge for us. Before the contract was up, Ringger Foods gained back all the money it had lost in previous years.

Another example of a "God-moment" was when we had an opportunity to make a significant cookie order for Nestlé. Before the product was to be released, we had scheduled a meeting with their quality assurance team. Minutes before they arrived, I received a call from my quality assurance director. She was in tears as she explained that a preliminary test on our product indicated listeria might have contaminated it. Listeria is bacteria that, in some cases, can cause death if ingested.

I remember walking into the conference room and meeting the Nestlé quality assurance team. I was emotional, shaken, and vulnerable, unsure of how they would react, but very transparent as I shared what had happened. Thankfully, they could not have been more helpful and they shared the steps that needed to be taken. The product was immediately put on hold until further testing could be done.

That night, I went home totally spent. In a case like this, the initial test could be wrong, so it would take an additional test to confirm the findings. I told Marla this could be the end of Ringger Foods. It was probably an overstatement but it was how I felt. After she tried to reassure me, I headed to the tub to relax, not knowing my Father would meet me there in a special way.

The previous night I had started reading a Readers' Digest article on prayer. Written from a secular viewpoint, researchers had found that in clinical tests at hospitals, patients who were prayed for recovered faster than those who were not prayed for. (Imagine that!) I picked up the article to finish reading it and literally within the first several paragraphs I read this: "Even more astounding are studies suggesting prayer can influence the growth of bacteria in a lab."[2]

I had never read anything like that before (or since) and it moved me to tears. Here I was, defeated and scared, waiting on the results of a lab test, and God speaks to me through a Reader's Digest article. What a personal Father God is! He knows everything about us and what we are going through. He knows the very number of hairs on my head. (Luke 12:7) He is in control of every situation.

I excitedly shared the article with Marla and called several friends to ask for their prayer support. Several days later we received word that the final test showed no signs of listeria. I still have the article and it is a remind-er to me who is really in control and that prayer does change things.

LESSONS LEARNED FROM THE FATHER

1. **Deep relationship requires time.** God loves us and wants to have a real and vibrant relationship with us. For any relationship to develop and deepen, you must spend time together.

2. **Effective prayer requires correct motives.** James 4:2-3 tells us, *"You don't have what you want because you don't ask God for it. And even when you ask, you don't get it because your motives are all wrong."* Before the contract, I had not spent a lot of time praying about busi-ness. To pray, "Dear Jesus, please make Ringger Foods successful so I can get rich and retire at 40" just didn't sound right. But now I was in a more tangible partner-ship with God. Now I was His steward. As a result, prayer became alive and powerful.

3. **God is a merciful Father and responds when we need Him.** When we are broken, and don't know what to do, we more urgently seek Him and cry out for His mercy. Psalm 33:22 says, *"Let thy mercy, O LORD, be upon us, according as we hope in thee."* Seeking mercy releases God's supernatural power on us.

4. **It's exciting to experience God's supernatural power.** When you are in a steward partnership with God, spending time with Him and seeking His wisdom and counsel, you experience Him in new and exciting ways!

THINGS TO CONSIDER

1. How is your prayer life? Is it the favorite time of your day?
2. Are you pleading with God for mercy? (Psalm 33:22)
3. Are you asking God for guidance on day to day decisions?
4. Are you experiencing answered prayer in real and specific ways? Are you asking with the right motives? Are you even asking at all? (James 4:2-3)

CHAPTER 3
COUNSEL

"Hello Gary, I'm sorry to have to tell you this, but your load was rejected."

"Rejected! Why?"

"Well, the buyer says it smells like fox urine."

Ringger Foods had made great progress with the Nutri-Sweet contract. It had turned our company around, dug us out of a financial hole in a relatively short time, and made me believe we were ready for a new level of success. I began looking for our next opportunity. Soon after the Nutri-Sweet contract expired, I met a gentleman who had a commercial food extruder and dryer for sale. He talked about all the potential food products that could be made with an extruder and even though he had not been successful himself I thought that, surely, I would be. Without much of a plan, I bought the equipment and then began exploring ways to use it.

About that time the oat bran "craze" hit. Oat bran was touted as the new miracle food. It supposedly could cure almost any ailment you had, from high cholesterol to cancer. I started researching how we could get into the oat bran game using our newly purchased extruder and dryer. To fully enter the game, we'd need more equipment, so, I put together a plan and started making purchases. Dad and Steph were both very concerned about these new expenses and cautioned me to slow down. They advised me to "walk before I run" and wanted me to be sure I knew what I was doing.

I was not to be deterred.

By nature I dislike confrontation, so I avoided further discussions. I believed this was an opportunity we needed to take advantage of and I plunged ahead. Before long I had a room filled with oat de-hullers, gravity tables, elevator legs, dust collectors and more. I was running fast and hard. Everything was going great according to my plan. Never mind the fact that due to my insufficient air exchange system, on a cold day the room fogged up so badly you couldn't see 20 feet ahead of you. I knew if we could do things quickly, success was just around the corner; we had a hungry market waiting. "If it's worth doing, it's worth doing wrong in the beginning" was my mantra.

The day finally arrived when we sold and shipped our first load of oat bran out east. This was a national market and pricing was good. We were on our way!

And then I got the call.

It was from the broker who'd arranged the sale. "Hello Gary, I'm sorry to have to tell you this, but your load was rejected."

"Rejected! Why?"

"Well, the buyer says it smells like fox urine."

I was flabbergasted. "Fox urine! How does he even know what fox urine smells like? You've got to be kidding me!"

But he wasn't kidding. And once again, reality hit.

What do you do when you have a rejected load of oat bran that smells like fox urine? You go on vacation. At least that's what I did. I remember walking along the beach, talking to Marla, wondering what was going to happen next. I knew an entrepreneur needed a certain amount of determination to do what he thinks is right, even when others around him don't agree. Stubborn determination was one of the things that had gotten me where I was. But this time I had taken it too far. Instead of listening to my team, I had plowed ahead even though they were telling me to slow down. God used this experience to teach me the truth of Proverbs 11:14 which says, *"In the multitude of counselors there is safety."* This became one of my life verses.

Because of all the new equipment I had purchased and the money lost in the "fox urine" fiasco, we were burning through large amounts of cash. Once again, I was seriously considering shutting down Ringger Foods and decided to share this with my vice president, Greg Umland. As I was contemplating how to tell him, Greg confided to me that doctors had diagnosed him with melanoma that could be life threatning. I went home heavy-hearted for him, wondering what to do. I remember standing in my bedroom, crying out in desperation, "Father I just can't say 'Hey Greg, I'm sorry about your cancer, and by the way, we're shutting down Ringger Foods.'" I was broken once again and reinforced my commitment that going forward I would listen to "the multitude of counselors".

God rewarded this new resolve in ways that were far above what I asked for or imagined.

First, and most importantly, Greg was treated and given a clean bill of health. In addition, we received a call from Quaker Oats that significantly changed Ringger Foods' outlook. Quaker Oats had a plant 90 miles away where they extruded crisp rice for their granola bars. They were planning to use their extrusion line for another purpose and needed to find a supplier to produce crisp rice. From the same small classified ad that gave us the lead with NutraSweet, Quaker found us. Our location was perfect and in time they offered us a contract.

Producing crisp rice required a lot of upgrades to our plant and this time I moved forward with a multitude of counsel. Dad, Steph, and Greg were excited and on board. We cleaned out my haphazard oat bran operation and with Quaker's guidance, started the journey of making Ringger Foods a first-rate ingredient supplier for the food industry. This partnership led to relationships with other nationally known food companies, and God once again showed how He brings beauty from ashes.

_____

LESSONS LEARNED FROM THE FATHER

1. **In the multitude of counselors there is safety.** It's human nature for the leader of a company to think he knows more than anyone else. After all, his blood, sweat, and tears are responsible for starting and making the business what it is. But sometimes he's too close to it and "can't see the forest for the trees." As I learned to ask for advice, God blessed me with numerous counselors; trusted friends who knew about Ringger Foods, but were far enough removed they could see things more clearly. I also learned to rely on my team, those close to the issues, who could offer valuable insights from their unique perspectives.

2. **There's strength in weakness.** I learned I didn't have to be right. In fact, I began to love it when an idea I started with completely changed through prayer and counsel. From my struggles, I developed a list of what I called "power verses," verses that encouraged and reminded me where my strength came from. Here are a few of them:

a. **2 Corinthians 12:9-10** *"Each time he said, 'My grace is all you need. My power works best in weakness.' So now I am glad to boast about my weaknesses, so that the power of Christ can work through me."*

b. **Isaiah 40:29** *"He gives power to the weak, and to those who have no might He increases strength."*

c. **Romans 9:16** *"It does not, therefore, depend on man's desire or effort, but on God's mercy."*

3. **Confrontation is opportunity.** I still tended to avoid conversations when I knew others would disagree with me. This often led to a lack of communication which frustrated my team. I remember listening to a self-help tape that focused on changing bad habits. The speaker had me visualize the next 1, 5, 10, and 20 years of not changing, continuing to do the same thing with the same negative results. Then he challenged me to create a new paradigm. I came up with the phrase "confrontation is opportunity" and it has stuck with me ever since. After all, if nothing changes, nothing changes and healthy confrontation leads to needed change. It's still hard for me to

confront someone, but now I believe it's an opportunity to bring unity and understanding.

4. **Use the LDL Method.** Confrontation can be productive, but if done in the wrong spirit it can also be lethal. When I have important conversations where strong and differing positions will be presented, I typically start the meeting with a brief explanation of a method I came up with to help navigate confrontation in a productive way. It goes something like this.

    a. **The first L stands for listen.** I want to listen carefully to each person as they share their ideas. At the same time, I want to listen to the Holy Spirit as we have our discussion.

    b. **The D stands for detached discernment.** In order to discern effectively, I need to be detached from my personal opinions so I can be objective and open to other ideas. I have learned that defensiveness gets in the way of seeing things clearly.

    c. **The last L stands for less.** Less of me. My opinions don't matter if they're not Spirit-led. If we can correctly discern His leading then we are all winners and that is our goal.

THINGS TO CONSIDER

1. Do you have counselors that you can bounce your ideas off of and get an honest response?
2. Are you encouraging open and honest discussion on business decisions – even when you know there will be strong feelings and disagreement?
3. In those discussions do you get defensive? If so, remember Listen – Discern – Less.

CHAPTER 4
FEAR(LESS)

"I'm mad at you!" I say to Marla as we drive by the Ringger Foods plant on our way to church.

"What! Why?" She exclaims.

"Because I have an offer to sell Ringger Foods and you're not at peace with it, so I can't do it!"

Ringger Foods was now producing crisp rice for three major food companies: Quaker Oats, M&M Mars and General Mills. Our increasing abilities and expertise had made us a credible and valued partner to their businesses, plus, there was potential for growth. We were becoming a recognized ingredient supplier throughout the industry.

The contract we made years ago was often in the back of my mind.

"If Ringger Foods ever becomes successful and we sell it, we will pay our investment back with interest; but the remaining balance will be used for Kingdom purposes."

How that would eventually play out was still a mystery to me, but as the business grew, I would think about the ramifications of it. I read a book by Bob Buford called Halftime[3]. The subtitle was "From Success to Significance." I loved that thought. Significance was something I wanted in my life and if I sold the business, Marla and I would be able to use the money to make a difference in God's Kingdom. This idea was sounding more and more compelling.

I was still enjoying Ringger Foods but there were times when I felt things could easily and quickly fall apart. Dad used to say, "Gary, those who have not owned a business don't understand the fine line between success and failure." I could relate. Some days it seemed Ringger Foods was going to be unbelievably successful, and the next day (or sometimes the next hour) I would wonder if it was all going to crash and burn.

With only three primary customers, if we lost one it would drastically change our cash flow. This often concerned me because of our operating loan. In addition, there was always the food safety risk. If a health problem occurred based on our product, the entire business was in jeopardy and again, I wondered if would we be able to pay off the loan.

We had employees working around the clock with lots of moving equipment. What if one of our employees was injured on the job? If I got a call in the evening or in the middle of the night, I would immediately tense up thinking something bad had happened. These thoughts often plagued me and I began to consider selling the business.

As Ringger Foods increased in value and legitimacy, we began receiving inquiries from firms interested in purchasing the company. The more offers we received, the more seriously I thought about selling. So, when an especially attractive purchase offer came for Ringger Foods, I decided to pursue it. We had several meetings with the interested party and I was becoming excited. This was a major decision, the type of decision that Marla and I had committed to make only if we both had peace about it.

The problem was, Marla was not catching the same vision and it irritated me. When calls came in the middle of the night, she didn't get the pit in her stomach. If we lost a customer, she wasn't the one who had to try to get a new one. She trusted me to run the business and though I appreciated her faith in me, I did not appreciate that she wasn't ready to sell. So, on our way to church one evening, I brought it up,

"I'm mad at you."

Startled, she looked at me, "What? Why?"

"I have an offer to sell Ringger Foods and because you're not at peace with it, I can't do it! You don't understand how much pressure is on me to keep it going."

Marla smiled, "Oh Gary, you'll figure it out!"

"Oh yeah," I said sarcastically, "Easy for you to say!"

The following week, I was on a plane to Texas, visiting the plant of one of our three main customers. Still searching for the answer at 30,000 feet, I was reading Chuck Swindoll's book The Mystery of God's Will[4]. In chapter 4, he shares this advice:

"Discovering and embracing God's will invariably brings us to a crisis of belief. And that forces us into faith and action. Obeying and delighting in God's will leads us to make major adjustments. And that requires us to release and risk - releasing the familiar and risking whatever the future may bring. That's the bottom line of fleshing out God's will."

As I read those words, 2 Timothy 1:7 came to mind, *"For God has not given us the spirit of fear but of power and of love and of a sound mind."* A wave of clarity rolled over me and I felt a sense of peace and direction. I knew God was speaking to me. My motive for selling was fear. Fear is not how God motivates His people. Fear originates with the enemy of our souls.

After visiting the plant that day, I had dinner, settled in at the hotel and called Marla.

"Hey Marla, I have something to tell you."

Before I could continue, she spoke up, "Wait, I have something to tell you first. Today I was listening to Focus on the Family's radio broadcast. Dr. Dobson was interviewing Chuck Swindoll..."

"Hmmm," I thought, "This is interesting."

"He was talking about how we need to be careful not to make decisions out of fear. He quoted the verse, 'God has not given us the spirit of fear; but of power and of love and of a sound mind.' And so, Gary," she said in a teasing voice, "I don't want you to be mad at me. I'll support whatever you decide, but I don't want you selling the business out of fear."

I shared what I had read on the plane, and we were both struck by this personal and special God-moment. Our heavenly Father used the same messenger, Chuck Swindoll, to unite us in the mutual conviction that this was not the time to sell Ringger Foods.

———

LESSONS LEARNED FROM THE FATHER

1. **God is a personal and caring Father.** Our heavenly Father has specific and exciting plans for us. *"For I know the plans I have for you," declares the LORD, "plans to prosper you and not to harm you, plans to give you a hope and a future."* (Jeremiah 29:11) We miss the best in life when we do our own thing instead of following His plan. His plan can be a mystery and sometimes hard to discern,

but He wants relationship and He wants us spending time with Him. If we seek Him out and give it time, God will give us clarity and direction. *"We can make our plans, but the LORD determines our steps."* (Proverbs 16:9)

2. **Fear is not from God.** 1 John 4:18 says, *"Perfect love casts out fear..."* With every major decision, there is a certain amount of angst. This doesn't mean you shouldn't use some healthy restraint and caution. I learned that from the fox urine experience. But if you are praying and asking God for direction, He will not use fear as the motivator.

3. **God wants us to be bold.** Proverbs 26:13 says, *"The lazy person claims, 'There's a lion on the road! Yes, I'm sure there's a lion out there.'"* I remember a time when I was talking with a Christian brother, sharing my business concerns and fears. Even though we didn't know each other well, I'll always remember that he said, "Keep taking risks." We need to be prudent, but we also need to remember that we have His Spirit working in us. *"I can do all things through Christ who strengthens me."* (Philippians 4:13)

4. God may lead us in a new direction. I understand why so many people live life in safe mode and never consider changing their career. Ringger Foods was where I spent most of my time, but I was still a 50% owner and the president of Ringger Feeds. I always thought I would stay involved in our family feed business the rest of my life. Then one day, Dad asked me to buy out his half. I realized I didn't have the ability to do that and continue growing Ringger Foods at the same time. His question forced me to consider deeply where I wanted to focus my time. Ultimately, I decided I should focus on Ringger Foods and we decided to sell Ringger Feeds. Sometimes He calls us to stay; sometimes He calls us to go. We must be open and submitted to His will and His plan for our lives. He knows best!

THINGS TO CONSIDER

1. Are you listening to your spouse (if you're married) and other counselors, or relying only on yourself?
2. Are you trusting God and asking him to guide you in making decisions?

3. Are you making decisions out of fear, or are you allowing God's peace to guide you?
4. Watch this Francis Chan video of the balance beam. It will amuse and challenge you! radicalbusiness.co/resources.

CHAPTER 5
PERFECT TIMING

"Hello Gary, this is Jack Warner of Kerry Foods. You don't know me but I know of you and if it's all right I'd like to have dinner with you at your convenience."

"Wow!" I thought, "If this is Kerry Foods calling to discuss buying Ringger Foods the timing is incredible!"

Ringger Foods was growing and it became clear that we needed a bigger and better facility to serve our customers. General Mills did an inspection and informed us if we would improve and add on to our facility we could continue to grow with them. If we didn't, they would find another supplier. We started considering different options that would satisfy their requirements.

In our small town there was a large food warehouse for sale that sat empty for several years. It was more space than we needed but Wayne Steffen, my project manager, checked it out anyway. He came back with a discouraging price: $3,300,000. It was way out of our range, so we decided our only option was to improve and add on to our current facility.

Upgrading our facility was a substantial investment. As we developed the construction plan, the added debt it would require concerned me. Up to this point, I was personally signing for all of Ringger Foods' debt. That meant if, for any reason, Ringger Foods could not repay the loan, our house, cars, and all personal assets would be liquidated to make further payments.

In Business by The Book[5], Larry Burkett cautions against personal signatures unless you have adequate assets to cover the note. I knew Ringger Foods had value but I also knew there were some risks beyond my control. I was convicted that I could not in good faith guarantee the new loan.

I decided to put a fleece before God. Judges 6:36-40 tells the account of Gideon and the fleece. He needed confirmation that God was really calling him to rescue Israel from their enemies.

Gideon said to God, *"If you are truly going to use me to rescue Israel as you promised, prove it to me in this way. I will put a wool fleece on the threshing floor tonight. If the fleece is wet with dew in the morning but the ground is dry, then I will know that you are going to help me rescue Israel as you promised."* And that is what happened. When Gideon got up early the next morning, he squeezed the fleece and wrung out a whole bowl full of water.

Then Gideon said to God, *"Please don't be angry with me, but let me make one more request. Let me use the fleece for one more test. This time let the fleece remain dry while the ground around it is wet with dew."* So that night God did as Gideon asked. The fleece was dry in the morning, but the ground was covered with dew.

In her Bible study book, Gideon, Priscilla Shirer says, *"I believe we can ask God for clarity in the face of challenge when our request comes from a true sense of faith – a faith that needs only to be strengthened."*[6] So, my fleece was this: If God wanted me to build a new addition, I would need a loan that did not require a personal guarantee. If I didn't find a bank willing to do that, then I would look for a buyer who had the financial ability to do what General Mills requested. Either way, I was at peace with the outcome. I met with numerous banks and after some diligent effort, I found a new bank that did not require my personal signature. They gave us a non-recourse loan and we improved our current plant and added a second facility to increase capacity. It was state-of-the-art.

True to their word, General Mills rewarded us with new business and we continued to grow. Two years later, Ringger Foods was once again running out of space and we needed to find a solution. It was a challenge, but as my dad would say, "Growing pains are better than dying pains."

Wayne decided to be proactive and without telling me, he checked with Fred Deal, a Realtor, on the price of the large warehouse in Gridley that was still sitting empty. Fred came back with a new price of $2,700,000. Wayne told him it was still too much and he wouldn't take that offer to me. He asked Fred to find out the owner's bottom line. The offer that came back shocked them both. In fact, Fred later told Wayne that in all his years in real estate, he never experienced anything like it. The offer was, if we could settle within 30 days, we could purchase the building for $750,000!

Wayne asked to have lunch with me that day so he could share this incredible development. What Wayne didn't know was that I had recently decided to redeem some stock to pay down debt. I had just received the check; it was sitting on my desk, still in the envelope. The amount of the check was just over $750,000! We both sensed God was providing an unusual opportunity for us, along with the necessary funds, at just the right time.

After lunch, Wayne and I went to check out the building. It was concrete, which was ideal for food production, and it was large, 150,000 square feet. In addition, approximately one third of it was cooler and freezer space. Buying this building would feel like we had made it to the big leagues. We both believed God arranged this opportunity and we accepted the offer.

Meanwhile, God was orchestrating other significant changes. The building deal happened in early September. Just prior to that, during our summer vacation, I had asked my family to pray for clarity if, and when, we should sell Ringger Foods. Even though exciting things were happening in the business, Marla and I reached a mutual peace that we should begin taking steps towards a possible sale. In October, I met with a consultant to get his advice and discuss potential opportunities. During that meeting, we considered two primary courses of action.

The first option was that I would find a business partner who would be able to infuse capital into Ringger Foods, someone who would also be my general manager. I had a gentleman in mind and I thought his addition to our company would allow me to spend my time focusing on new ideas and growing the business. It would also give me some margin to start exploring ministry ideas.

The second option was to sell the business. The consultant knew the food industry well and we listed several companies who would strategically benefit by acquiring Ringger Foods. An Irish company called Kerry Foods was at the top of the list. Kerry was active in the U.S. and had made numerous acquisitions of industrial food companies like us.

We both agreed that I should check out the first option, so I immediately made an appointment with the gentleman I had in mind to be my business partner. We met the next Friday and had a good discussion, but when I left I was disappointed. I knew in my gut it was not a good fit. On the way home, I checked my voice mail. I still remember my exact location when I heard the unexpected message. I was humbled as I listened. It felt like another personal touch from God.

"Hello Gary, this is Jack Warner of Kerry Foods. You don't know me but I know of you, and if it's all right I'd like to have dinner with you at your convenience."

Kerry Foods is a large company and I didn't know Jack's position or title. For all I knew, he could have been a sales agent trying to sell us something. Regardless, I immediately shared his message with Marla and Dad when I got home. I knew if Jack was senior management and offering to acquire us, the timing was incredible. We agreed I had no choice but to follow through and see if God was opening a door in a very special way.

On Monday, I called Jack, found out he was the CEO of Kerry North America and he was, in fact, interested in purchasing Ringger Foods. We set up a meeting for the end of the week.

I prepared some general financial information with future projections. At the meeting, we discussed our goals and timing and before I left, we had a general handshake agreement of what the price would be. Jack said he would come to Gridley with a team to "kick the tires" and if that went well, he would give us a formal offer.

Within a week, his team visited our plant. It was exciting to show them around. We could tell they were impressed with Ringger Foods. It was also clear that our new production facility appealed to them. I didn't know it then, but this was a future blessing for my employees. In time, Kerry moved other manufacturing processes from outdated plants they owned to our new plant. Selling at God's perfect timing gave my employees opportunities I never could have provided.

The following week, Jack sent me a formal offer. We had one additional meeting and signed off on the sale. Within two months, from start to finish, the deal was completed. The Kerry legal team told us they had never experienced a sale process moving so smoothly and quickly. Our newly purchased building was not included in the sale, but the agreement did include a substantial lease for warehouse space within the building.

As we reviewed these events, we marveled at how God arranged it all. Based on the new production facility and the added General Mills business, the value of Ringger Foods was now substantially more than it was when I previously considered selling.

But the rest of the story is a tribute to God's mercy and to Marla, whose lack of peace prevented me from accepting that first offer. The first company I had considered selling to offered an initial payment that would be followed by additional payments based on future financial results. Soon after we declined their offer, that company declared bankruptcy. If we had accepted their offer, we would have never received any of those payments!

Kerry, on the other hand, paid us 100% at closing, a cash payment that was over five times what we would have received if we had sold two years earlier. This higher price along with our purchase of the warehouse building would provide multiple ministry and business opportunities in the future. Even though we couldn't see it yet, God was preparing our way.

LESSONS LEARNED FROM THE FATHER

1. Don't rush things. Let God lead you. He knows all things and He has a plan. Through the years, I've learned to listen and wait to act until I feel His urgency and leading, confirmed with peace.

2. Don't guarantee debt you can't guarantee. James 4:13-14 says, *"Look here, you who say, 'Today or tomorrow we are going to a certain town and will stay there a year. We will do business there and make a profit.' How do you know what your life will be like tomorrow?'"* Conservative, prudent debt is a useful tool if it is backed up with proper collateral. But many of us get sucked into bondage by personally guaranteeing loans reliant on future events we don't fully control. Before signing, surrender it to the Father. If He wants you to move forward in a new business opportunity, and if you are willing to put forth the effort, He will provide the right banking or business relationship needed.

3. Trust that God will prepare your way. Esther never dreamed she would become Queen of Persia as a young Jewish girl, but God had a plan. He used her to save her people from annihilation. As her cousin Mordecai reflected, she had been placed *"for such a time as this."* (Esther 4:14) God had a plan for Esther and He has a purpose and plan for you and me today.

THINGS TO CONSIDER

1. Are you waiting on God or running ahead of Him making your own decisions?
2. Have you guaranteed or are you considering guaranteeing a debt that you cannot repay if things go wrong? Surrender it to God and ask Him what to do.
3. Reflect on an experience when you let God lead, and an experience when you went ahead of Him. Resolve to follow His lead from now on.

CHAPTER 6
LIFESONG FOR ORPHANS

"How do I use this money?" I asked Clayt.

"Don't just write checks," replied my friend and mentor, "Be focused and involved. And dream BIG. That way, if it happens, you'll know it was God and not you!"

After the Ringger Foods closing, Marla and I began to pray for wisdom on how to move forward. We also sought advice from our "multitude of counselors."

One counselor was my friend and mentor Clayton Irmeger. Clayt was older and wiser and had been involved in direct ministry most of his life. When I asked for his thoughts on how to use the proceeds from the sale, he gave me advice that I have shared with others many times since. "Be focused and involved. Don't just share your money; share your passion, time and talents. And dream BIG. That way, if it happens, you'll know it was God and not you."

Clayt's advice resonated with me. I wanted to focus on an area where I could use the gifts, skills and experiences God had given me, but the vast number of good ministries to choose from was overwhelming. In a world with so many needs, what ministry should we focus on?

As we pondered this, we recalled a conversation Marla had years ago with Marie, one of her friends at church. Marie and her husband were in the process of adopting a little boy from South Korea. She was unable to have children biologically and was excitedly sharing how God had called them to this important step. She also shared with Marla how much the adoption was going to cost. They were planning to take out a loan to pay for it.

When Marla came home from church that day she told me, "Gary, no young couple should have to go into debt to adopt. We need to help them." We were grateful we could bless this young couple financially. When we saw that little boy in church each Sunday, we were blessed even more, knowing we had played a supporting role in bringing him home.

As we reflected on that experience, the thought of helping more families adopt was exciting to us. We saw how the theme of adoption is prevalent throughout the Gospel. As followers of Christ, we have been adopted into God's forever family. We were convicted as we read Scripture sharing God's heart for the fatherless. Verses like James 1:27, *"Pure and genuine religion in the sight of God the Father means caring for orphans and widows in their distress"* and Psalm 68:6, *"God sets the lonely in families."* became more urgent and personal to us. It was becoming clear. We believed God was telling us to help Christian families defray the high cost of adoption.

From a business perspective, it made a lot of sense to me. What could be better than helping an orphan find a "forever" family? Adoptions were expensive but once the child was in the home, there would be no ongoing ministry costs as the family would take care of the child's needs. If we could help them overcome the initial financial hurdle, more children would be adopted into loving homes. We believed this was a high impact way to use the funds God had entrusted to us.

Our mission was set. Now we needed to make it happen. My first step was to find the right person to help administrate this work. Clint, my son-in-law, told me Andy Lehman was looking for a job. Andy and his wife, Jill, had been house-parents at a children's home in Indiana and had decided it was time to move back, closer to family. I knew and respected Andy as a godly young man so I arranged a meeting with him and Jill. As we discussed our dream of helping families adopt, it seemed like a natural fit. They had served at a children's home and were now planning to adopt themselves. They would soon be experiencing the adoption journey first-hand and we felt a mutual peace about moving ahead together. I offered Andy the job.

I was just in time.

Prior to our conversation, Andy had applied for a job with his former employer. He was initially turned down as the company had a hiring freeze. The day after our conversation, his former boss contacted him; he had been given special permission to hire Andy and offered him a job. It was a good job, one that Andy and Jill had hoped for. But now, they felt God was calling them in a new direction. Once again God's perfect timing was at work — He was building a team to reach the fatherless.

Andy started meeting with adoptive couples who needed financial assistance. It wasn't long before we had more couples applying than we had funds to help. I specifically remember one family who had twelve children, nine of them adopted, and several with special needs. They were not wealthy but they were committed to making a difference. It was a privilege to come along side of them and other godly families who were bringing hope and family to lost children.

And then we met Patricia Busby, founder of a ministry called Life International. Life International distributed blankets and other essential items to orphanages in Ukraine. Denis Poshelok was a young Ukrainian who helped her carry out this mission. The Soviet government built these orphanages in the 1940s and Denis personally knew parents whose children were taken from them and placed there. According to the government, these parents were "unfit" to raise their own children due to their Christian faith. Now God was at work bringing beauty from ashes. He was giving Denis a vision that would impact the lives of children living in these orphanages in a deep way. Denis called this vision Constant Christian Presence (CCP).

Patricia could see Denis' vision developing and realized she could only offer limited support. She was praying God would provide someone to take over the ministry and when she heard about our work supporting adoptions, she asked us to visit Ukraine to meet Denis and see the need. We accepted her invitation.

This was our first trip to eastern Europe. I remember getting off the plane and seeing soldiers standing on the runway with machine guns, an ominous first impression. Traveling through the city, we reflected how everything looked gray and bleak; the buildings, the sky, the roads, the people. The next two days we visited orphanages full of beautiful sweet children, but the hopelessness was palpable. We felt sick at heart and overwhelmed with the needs. It was beginning to affect our emotions and by the third night, Marla and I were discouraged. We lay in bed that night while loud Ukrainian music played outside our hotel. We couldn't sleep; we just wanted to go home.

Then came the morning.

We left our hotel and drove to Izume Orphanage where we saw the pilot project of Denis' CCP model. Denis had worked out a long-term lease agreement with the orphanage director that allowed his team to fix up one room they called the "Room of Hope and Trust." While the rest of the orphanage was dark and dreary, the Room of Hope and Trust was bright, cheery and inviting.

Denis had hired Slavic and Natasha, a young married couple from the local church in Izume, to develop the CCP Program. It was obvious they put their heart and soul into it. In the Room of Hope and Trust, Slavic and Natasha conducted daily Vacation Bible School activities. I was reminded of my Sunday School days as Natasha shared Bible stories using a felt board with paper characters. We also learned how they were personally mentoring the kids. Slavic would take the boys fishing and Natasha was teaching the girls to sew. They were loving them and teaching them about Jesus and the kids were responding.

Before we left that day, the kids put on a program for us. As they sang songs, Denis was translating their words in my ear. They were singing praise to Jesus in a state run Eastern bloc orphanage formerly used to separate children from Christian parents! That day totally changed our perspectives about getting involved with Denis and his team. We believed God was calling us to help, but were unsure how. We knew we had a lot of praying to do.

Back home, reality set in. More and more requests were coming in from adoptive families and now we were considering adding an orphan ministry in Ukraine. We didn't have enough resources to do both unless we asked others for help. This was too big! Fundraising was never in our plan. Asking others for money sounded hard. I was a businessman. I didn't ask for money, I made money!

Once again God had to break me. I remember a specific time during the seven-mile drive from our home to the office. So many thoughts were coming at me. I believed in our adoption ministry, I believed in Denis and the vision God had given him, but I didn't know how to do both. As I struggled with what to do, a Rich Mullins' song began playing on my CD player, "Hold me Jesus, I'm shaking like a leaf, you have been king of my glory, won't you be my prince of peace." In that moment, I felt the Holy Spirit saying, "You have spiritual pride about YOUR family foundation. This is not about your family, this is about MY family. You need to let go and let God." That short drive was a turning point for me.

As I shared my fundraising concerns with Dad, he said, "Gary, you don't have to twist people's arms. Simply share the story." Marla and I appreciated the wisdom of those words; they gave us the encouragement and freedom we needed to take over Life International, later to be called Lifesong for Orphans. It was the beginning of a beautiful journey full of twists and turns, challenges and blessings.

———

LESSONS LEARNED FROM THE FATHER

1. **The mind of man plans his way, but the Lord directs his steps.** (Proverbs 16:9) My initial goal was to create a family foundation. I wanted a meaningful project that would unite us, but Lifesong has given our family more opportunities than my plan could have ever provided. (More on this in chapter 7)

2. **It's exciting to be on God's team.** We have experienced the joy of a much bigger family in the body of Christ. We've been privileged to meet so many inspiring people and have learned first-hand how our many different gifts can blend together for more effective ministry.

3. Join the movement. In Experiencing God[7], Henry Black-aby advises to watch where God is moving and join Him in that movement instead of starting your own initiative. We feel like we've had a front row seat, watching the movement God is creating in His church. Children are being adopted, mentored, and cared for because the church is answering the call to make a difference.

THINGS TO CONSIDER

1. Is there a ministry God has specifically called you to?
2. Does Clayt's advice resonate to you?
    a. Be focused and involved. Share your time, talents and treasure.
    b. Dream big. Then if your dream happens, recognize it was God and not you.
3. Are you letting go and letting God? Do you hold your goals loosely with an open hand — always open to His direction?

CHAPTER 7
FAMILY MISSION

"The contract changed everything" I said to Megan. "I wouldn't have my "Moonshine" (a pet-name for my granddaughter Suhn).

Megan's eyes teared up as she reflected on how different our lives would have been had they not adopted Suhn eight years prior.

Making the contract with God affected our family in significant ways. Although we started an adoption ministry, Marla and I never adopted. However, our three daughters have caught the vision. Of our 15 grandchildren, nine are adopted. This is a special chapter to me as I've asked the four key women in my life to share how their lives have been affected by the contract. Here are their thoughts:

MARLA (MY BETTER HALF)

When I think about the contract Gary made with God all those years ago that eventually led to Lifesong for Orphans, I can't help thinking what I would have missed if he had not signed it. The last lines of Robert Frost's poem, The Road Not Taken, sum it up perfectly:

"Two roads diverged in a wood and I, I took the one less traveled by and that has made all the difference."

Adoption, foster care, and orphan care were simply words I read about when I was younger. After we became involved in orphan ministry, those words became personal.

Before, the idea of adoption made me feel unsettled, even a little scared. So, you can imagine how I felt when my oldest daughter, Megan and her husband Kory were considering special needs adoptions. Or how anxious I was when our middle daughter, Jami and her husband Clint adopted through the foster care system. Or my hesitation when Leslie, our youngest daughter, believed God was calling her to bring two teenage girls from Zambia into her home. But God put all my fears to rest as each child was introduced to our family through adoption.

My children have become my heroes. They have opened their hearts and homes to kids who needed forever families and I am a better person because of it. I have learned that orphans, no matter their color or age or special need, are just children who need someone to believe in them. I get emotional when I think of not being grandma to those nine precious kids who have joined our family.

Being part of an orphan ministry has drastically changed my perspective on the Body of Christ. It is SO much bigger than the box I had it in. I have had the opportunity to read amazing testimonies of faith from adoptive parents across the United States, to meet missionaries who are sacrificing to follow God's call, and to see first-hand the work being done in third world countries by nationals who want to make their community a better place for their children. I am blessed to know them and to call them my friends.

Working alongside Gary at Lifesong, spending time doing something we both believe in, has made us closer as a couple. When I was in my 40s, I spent a lot of time praying about my purpose. My girls were grown (or almost grown) and I was feeling restless, wanting to do something more with my time. After we started the ministry, without realizing it, I was no longer praying about what to do. Whether it was in the office processing applications from adoptive parents, at home babysitting my grandchildren, or across the world on a vision trip, I was helping to serve orphans. I had found my purpose.

Life with Gary has had its moments, both good and bad, but it has never been boring. He has taken risks in business throughout our marriage and I have almost always supported him. When he signed the contract with God,

I was on board 100%. Little did I know the joys it would bring to our marriage. It has been a wonderful journey, at times exhilarating and at times heartbreaking. I am thankful for the ride.

MEGAN (FIRSTBORN)

I don't remember when Dad first made the contract; I was only a kid.

I don't remember much about the beginning of Lifesong, either. I was a newlywed at the time living in the city. I'm sure I was supportive and excited to see how God was leading my parents. I'm also sure we had conversations with them about the direction God was leading them, but I don't remember the specific moments. I do, however, remember being part of the first mission trip Lifesong took to Ukraine. That is something I will never forget.

Kory and I left our one-year-old baby girl at home to travel with my parents and a group of college students to help run a Vacation Bible School at an orphanage in Ukraine. I remember landing in Kharkov to gray everything and soldiers with guns. I think at one point, Kory was pulled into a dark room by the soldiers and asked questions in Russian that he couldn't understand. I remember bouncing over dirt roads to a run-down manor-type building with overgrown grasses and weeds where we held the camp. Mostly, I remember the kids, one in particular, named Valya.

My most vivid memory with Valya took place just before she was going to perform in a skit with several of the other kids. I remember arriving at the stage just as they were beginning their performance; she was anxiously looking around until she saw me. Then she smiled and began to perform.

It was a small moment, but one I think of often. Every time my kids perform in a Sunday school program and look for me, I think of Valya and the millions of other kids who don't have a parent there to watch THEM as they perform.

That trip and that moment was impactful for our family-to-be. I think we may have adopted without it, but I know that seeing kids without families first-hand, interacting with them, observing where they lived and slept, solidified in our hearts the desire to adopt. We saw hundreds of kids needing families and though we couldn't help them all, we could offer our family to a few.

Since that trip, we have gone through the adoption process twice and were able to fund both adoptions with the help of Lifesong and the generosity of family and friends. Our family looks a little different than how I once thought it might. It is multi-cultural and includes two kids with special needs. Adoption has challenged us and blessed us in more ways than we can count.

I am thankful for the journey God led my dad on beginning with that contract so many years ago. I am thankful for the real life example my parents have been of what it looks like to follow Jesus in a radical way. And I am thankful for the impact Lifesong has made on our lives and many others.

JAMI (MIDDLE CHILD)

When I was a child, my dad went through a season of depression but honestly, I don't remember that. I do remember going on dates with him, his ability to make me laugh, and listening to him sing us to sleep at night. And, I remember watching him pray.

He would sit in his hot tub where he would talk, dream, and just hang out with the Lord.

Seeing him pray like this impacted me deeply. I saw him model real relationship with Jesus and it was compelling.

When we were first married, my husband Clint and I never considered adoption or foster care. In fact, it scared me, like sick-to-my-stomach-when-I-thought-about-it scared. But when my parents started Lifesong, I began to see the world in a different way. I watched friends adopting children from different countries, many with the help of Lifesong grants. Getting to know these kids took away some of that fear and opened our eyes to the idea of adoption.

This awareness prompted a curiosity that compelled Clint and me to pray. As we prayed we became available and open to whatever God would ask of us. And then action followed. I am now a mom of seven children, five through adoption, both international adoption and through the foster care system.

During our foster care journey, I remember Dad saying, "Jami, I think this foster care thing might be bigger than you and your family. It makes me wonder why Lifesong isn't involved in foster care."

Clint and I both sensed the Lord at work, creating a vision in my heart for something more. This vision materialized and became The Forgotten Initiative (TFI) in April of 2011. TFI is a ministry dedicated to mobilizing the church by connecting it to the needs of those who feel forgotten in the foster care community.

With support from Dad, Lifesong brought us under their wing and continues to serve us today with accounting, coaching and more. Because of Lifesong, TFI has been able to do more than we could have alone.

I'm so thankful for Lifesong for Orphans. Not only have they strengthened TFI's efforts, they also helped us with our adoptions. It's a tremendous blessing (and just plain fun!) to serve alongside my Dad and watch him live out this adventure.

LESLIE (YOUNGEST)

I was just a toddler when my dad made the contract with God. I have heard the story so many times that it feels almost like a memory, though I know I was too young to remember it. But, I do remember how the dynamic in our house shifted when Dad sold Ringger Foods and my parents caught the vision to help the vulnerable and orphaned.

As a 17-year old, I cared very little how involved my parents were in the financial aspect of anything. My mind would often go a little numb, and I would internally whimper from boredom when Dad began to talk about money matters and spreadsheets. (For the record, I have grown to appreciate his love relationship with spreadsheets and have even created my own on occasion.) But I was immediately excited about the ministry, feeling it was a great thing for our family. I loved seeing my dad light up when he talked about how intentionally God was leading and what he was learning from it all.

During my freshman year in college, the ministry began to extend beyond adoption financial assistance. When it crossed the ocean to help indigenous people care for orphans in their own exotic lands, like Ukraine, India, Ethiopia and Zambia, it began to appeal to me in an entirely new way. I jumped at the opportunity to be "supportive" and offered my time to travel with or for them whenever possible.

In my late 20s, I worked with Lifesong for a few years, both in their office and abroad. Through it all, God was faithfully directing me in my own journey. I remember during that period, amidst the turmoil of transition and searching for my purpose, reading these words by Oswald Chambers in My Utmost for His Highest[8]:

Perseverance means more than endurance. A saint's life is in the hands of God like a bow and arrow in the hands of an archer. God is aiming at something the saint cannot see, and He stretches and strains, and every now and again the saint says, "I cannot stand anymore." God does not heed, He goes on stretching until His purpose is in sight, and then He lets fly. Trust yourself to God's hands.

Today, I am in year three of hosting two former students of mine, from when I taught at Lifesong School-Zambia, as they pursue a high school education here in the States. I started working toward a Masters of Art in counseling after living abroad and seeing the need for mental health professionals to better serve missionaries. To say I am living a life I never would have planned for myself would be an understatement of hilarious proportions. Yet here we are. I have seen God's purpose "let fly" in my family through adoption, ministry, and in my own life. None of it has been particularly easy, but His purpose has always been worth it.

———

LESSONS LEARNED FROM THE FATHER

1. **Pure religion binds us together.** There are many great causes and ways we can serve our Father. However, I don't know of any that has a higher endorsement from the Bible than serving orphans. Isaiah 1:17 says, *"defend the fatherless."* Psalm 146: 9 states, "*He cares for the orphans and widows.*" I've seen families struggle as they debate theology, but in my experience, caring for orphans unifies. We become the hands and feet of Jesus as we care for them. James 1:27 says, *"pure religion is caring for orphans."* An adoptive parent once told me that verse is not a commandment, but a definition. So, if you want to draw together as a family and experience pure religion, take care of orphans and vulnerable children.

2. **Ministering together blessed our marriage.** The contract was the stimulus that ultimately allowed Marla and me to work together in a deeper and more meaningful way. After the kids were gone, she was struggling with purpose. Had I pursued the American Dream, I would have been struggling with purpose and contentment as

well. Thankfully, because of the commitment to use our talents and treasure for His work, we enjoy greater joy and purpose together.

3. **Ministering together blessed our family.** God used the contract and the resulting Lifesong journey to change not only me and Marla, but our children as well. Better yet, I see it affecting my grandchildren. I hear them talking about growing up to be a missionary, adopting or wanting to visit an international Lifesong project. These are things I never thought about as a kid. Luke 1:50 states, *"His mercy extends to those who fear him, from generation to generation."* And as John said in 3 John verse 4, *"nothing gives me greater joy than my children walking in truth."* I believe this journey changed my family for generations to come and that gives me great joy.

4. **Our grandkids have made us "color-blind."** Though Marla and I never adopted, I do remember considering it. It is almost amusing to me (and somewhat embarrassing) that as we considered adoption years ago, I was interested in adopting from Russia primarily because

then our child would look more like us. As Marla stated, we have both learned that orphans, no matter their color or age or special need, are just children who need someone to believe in them. Our grandkids come in many shapes, sizes, and colors and they all fit perfectly into our family.

THINGS TO CONSIDER

1. Is your work or business enhancing or detracting from your role as a godly spouse or parent?
2. Does your work or business draw your children toward God?
3. If God were to call you home now, would you regret how you prioritized your family and friends?
4. How can you change your work-life so that it more effectively draws your family closer to God and each other?
5. Is there a ministry that you and your family could get involved with together to make a difference?

PART 3

THE CHALLENGE

CHAPTER 8
GET RADICAL!

Years ago, I remember listening to Dad and a new Christian discuss the word "radical." The young man expressed how he wanted to be radical for Christ and Dad questioned if that was the right word. To him, radical had a negative connotation. I typically agree with Dad, but in this case, I think he had it wrong. I want to be radical for Christ. The dictionary states that radical means "very different from the usual; associated with policies of extreme change." Isn't that what Jesus was about? Isn't that what we want to be about: making change for the better?

God had to break me before I embraced a new and radical view of business. But it doesn't have to be that way for you.

It wasn't that way for Alan Barnhart. Alan met his wife, Katherine at the University of Tennessee. Part of what drew them together was their mutual desire to be missionaries.

Shortly after their marriage, Alan's dad threw them a curve ball. He made them an offer to take over the family construction business. This was a special offer and a position that Alan was uniquely qualified to fulfill. But it was clearly a different path than he and Katherine had planned. They started to pray about which direction God had for them. Initially, in Alan's words, each time they tried to make their decision "the vote came out one to one."

In time, they reached a mutual decision to go forward in business but they purposed in their hearts to keep their missionary mindset, choosing to live a modest lifestyle. Alan, Katherine and Alan's brother all agreed to cap their income even if the business prospered. They did not want to increase their lifestyle, they wanted to increase their giving. Jesus' warnings about how money can corrupt and keep us from eternal life weighed heavily on them so they shared their commitment to others to keep themselves accountable.

That commitment was made in 1986 and God blessed their business above and beyond their expectations. Barnhart Crane and Rigging, having consistently grown year after year for over 30 years, now gives millions of dollars away each year. The employees know and appreciate that their work is more than a job and a living. Their combined efforts are making a lasting and profound difference in God's Kingdom.[9]

Jesus understood the temptation of wealth when he spoke to his disciples in Matthew 13.

He said, *"Now listen to the explanation of the parable about the farmer planting seeds: The seed that fell among the thorns represents those who hear God's word, but all too quickly the message is crowded out by the worries of this life and the lure of wealth, so no fruit is produced. The seed that fell on good soil represents those who truly hear and understand God's Word and produce a harvest of thirty, sixty, or even a hundred times more!"*

His message was clear. We are to use our gifts and talents for His work. If we use them for ourselves, no lasting fruit is produced. If we use them for Him then, by His grace, we can produce a harvest of thirty, sixty, or even a hundred times more!

———

THINGS TO CONSIDER

Is God calling you to do business in a new and radical way? While I don't claim to have all the answers, I've been blessed with some great partners and coaches. Here are a few ideas to get you started.

1. **Like the Barnhart's, adopt a business missionary mindset.** In Mark 10, Jesus looked around and said to his disciples, *"How hard it is for the rich to enter the Kingdom of God!"* This amazed them. But Jesus said again, *"Dear children, it is very hard to enter the Kingdom of God. In fact, it is easier for a camel to go through the eye of a needle than for a rich person to enter the Kingdom of God!"*

Scriptures like this gave the Barnharts a healthy fear and respect for the deceptive power of money. Regardless of their business success, they wanted to live modestly much like they would have done as missionaries.

Ask God to give you a fear and respect for the power of money. Then, prayerfully develop and commit to a standard of living and give the rest away. Develop this "finish line" commitment in counsel with your spouse and other advisors. Write it down and ask them to hold you accountable.

2. **Reject the tithe generosity myth.** Our original giving plan at Ringger Feeds and Ringger Foods was post-tax tithing. We felt it was a biblical directive and that by doing so we were being generous.

I don't think we had it quite right.

When tithing is discussed in the Bible, it's based on gross income (10% of their crop), not post-tax income. And it's only mentioned by Jesus when he was referring to, or talking with Pharisees, not exactly the model we want to follow.

Let's not put God's will for our giving in a box. Depending on our financial situation, tithing may in fact be very generous. Or it may be a small "tip" that is much less than our Father deserves and expects. The key is to give willingly and sacrificially as did the widow who gave two small coins.

"I tell you the truth, this poor widow has given more than all the others who are making contributions. For they gave a tiny part of their surplus, but she, poor as she is, has given everything she had to live on." (Luke 21:3)

3. **Embrace God's Giving Law.** Jesus said *"Give, and you will receive. Your gift will return to you in full–pressed down, shaken together to make room for more, running over, and poured into your lap. The amount you give will determine the amount you get back."* (Luke 6:38)

I've learned this doesn't mean you can make bad business decisions and expect good results. But, I have experienced God's special mercy with my businesses based on the contract commitment and I believe He blesses businesses whose purpose is to give back. I call it God's giving law. *"The amount you give will determine the amount you get back."*

4. **Develop a "triple bottom line" business plan.** I learned this strategy from Generous Giving (generousgiving.org). The first bottom line is your profit. The second bottom line is how much you give away. The third bottom line is how you treat your employees, suppliers, and customers. Treating customers with respect and dignity is relatively easy. Treating employees and suppliers in a Christ-like way is a greater challenge, but it is a tremendous discipleship opportunity. Once again, we release a special power based on Jesus' prayer when He said, *"I am praying not only for these disciples but also for all who will ever believe in me through their message."* (John 17:20) The way you conduct business at every level should create an atmosphere where you can share Jesus Christ.

5. **Find a key ministry that your business supports and involve your team.** Watershed Foods is a company that

has named Lifesong for Orphans as its featured ministry. Several times per year, Lifesong gives updates to the Watershed employee team and thanks them for making a difference around the world. After a consultant conducted an employee survey for Watershed, he told me 100% of the survey group responded that knowing they were making a difference for children added to their job satisfaction. It's a well-documented fact that employees who believe there is purpose in their work are more content. Whatever ministry you support, make it real to your employees. They will think differently about their jobs and it will have a positive effect on them, your business and the ministry you serve.

6. **Collaborate with a group of like-minded partners.**
Lifesong has taught me so much about how big and powerful the body of Christ is. God has brought partners into our lives who have helped us serve orphans and are also helping us do more in business in two primary ways.

a. **Sustainable Business.** We all know the old proverb *"Give a man a fish and you'll feed him for a day. Teach a man to fish and you'll feed him for a lifetime."*

At Lifesong we're creating in-country businesses to help the kids we serve to thrive as they enter adulthood. We also have the goal that the business will ultimately make the ministry operations self-sustainable. You can visit lifesongfarms.org to learn and to inspire new ideas for you and your team.

b. **Impact Business.** At Lifesong we have a 100% Pledge. This means when a donor gives, whether it's to help a family adopt, to support an international school, or to support foster care, 100% of their donation goes to ministry, with no administrative costs taken out. We can do this because of the financial support of a small group of businessmen and women who are committed to helping us sustain this pledge. We are working together to develop what we call "business giving engines." To learn about these strategies, visit lifesongimpact.org.

I've found when the primary business purpose is to further the Gospel, personal negotiating and taxes go *down*, while doors open *up* for partnerships to develop in unusual ways.

7. Get acquainted with National Christian Foundation (NCF) and Impact Foundation (nationalchristianfounda-tion.org and impactfoundation.org). These foundations are set up to help Christian businessmen and women give money away more effectively. They have proven methods to help you save substantial tax dollars making it possible to give more away and still have money left to pay yourself well and reinvest in your business. Both organizations have private letter rulings that give their methods approval from the IRS.

8. Join the ongoing discussion at radicalbusiness.co. Here you can find additional resources, like tips to set your own finish line and spreadsheet templates that calculate how NCF and Impact Foundation can help you give more effectively. You can also share with and learn from other like-minded businessmen and women. Let's learn together and create more radical businesses for His glory.

9. Most importantly, develop and deepen your rela-tionship with Jesus. If your business goals are to serve Him, if you are His steward, then He is truly your

business partner. Talk with Him daily. Ask Him what to do about business decisions. Take time to sit and listen for His response. You will experience Him guiding you in ways that are "more than you can ask or imagine." (Ephesians 3:20)

FINAL THOUGHTS

In recent years, business has gotten a bad rap. Some circles have looked down on it as a selfish and shallow ambition and sometimes it is. But don't let that dampen your excitement about the radical business plan God has for you. If you have business ability and passion, it's a gift from God. Use it *"to serve others, as faithful stewards of God's grace."* (1 Peter 4:10)

I believe God is moving His church toward a new and radical business mindset. I see it in millennials who, more than my generation, want their work to be about mission. I see it in my peers who would rather invest in a giving engine than continually give to an ongoing need.

Perhaps you are like Esther, someone equipped with special gifts and skills for "such a time as this." My prayer is that God will use this book in some small way to help you step out and answer His call. If you do, I promise you it will be quite a ride.

I did not trust Him, at first, in control of my life.
I thought He'd wreck it; but he knows bike secrets,
knows how to make it bend to make sharp corners,
knows how to jump to clear high rocks, knows how to
fly to shorten scary passages.

And I am learning to shut up and pedal in the strangest
places, and I'm beginning to enjoy the view,
and the cool breeze on my face, with my delightful
constant companion, Jesus Christ.

And when I'm sure I can't do anymore,
He just smiles and says ... "Pedal."

ABOUT THE AUTHOR

Although Gary serves as president of Lifesong for Orphans, his preferred title is Orphan Advocate. His passion is developing radical businesses to create "perpetual giving engines" and employment opportunities for orphans and vulnerable children. He has the blessing of being an entrepreneur (which sometimes when running unchecked becomes a curse) and has been involved (at last count) in 11 start-ups. Gary has been married to Marla for 41 years and they have been blessed with 3 children and 15 grandchildren.

ABOUT LIFESONG FOR ORPHANS

Currently, Lifesong has helped bring over 7,000 children home to forever families. Lifesong also serves approximately 9,000 vulnerable children in foster and orphan care ministries around the world.

Because of its "roots," Lifesong is uniquely involved in business in two primary ways.

- Sustainable businesses which empower indigenous advocates to give orphans employment and make in-country ministries sustainable without on-going support.
- Impact businesses which give donors the opportunity to invest in domestic businesses that are "perpetual giving engines" (for Lifesong and other ministries).

THANKS TO

- Dad for introducing me to business and guiding me along the way. I still use so many of your quotes when I share ideas.
- The Ringger Feeds team who put up with all my good and bad ideas and cleaned up the messes I created. You are the reason I learned to love business.
- The Ringger Foods team who paved the way for Lifesong for Orphans. Special thanks to Greg who was with me from the beginning and for his help in landing the major accounts. And to Wayne who was and continues to be my mentor.
- Jeremy for rescuing Watershed Foods when it was faltering; and Steve for starting Gobena and Element; to Luke for taking Gobena from its foundation to a new level.
- The Lifesong team of advocates who serve children in remarkable ways. Special thanks to Andy who was with me from the beginning and continues to help shape the size and scope of our ministry. And to Patricia and

Denis who initiated our journey from a family foundation to Lifesong.

- Marla, Megan, Jami, and Leslie, my sons-in-law Kory and Clint, and my 15 grandkids who all love me and even like me. And as Dad says (to quote him one more time) "Like is better than love. Love is a commandment but like is voluntary."

- My book team: Marla and Megan who turned ramblings, dashes, ...'s, and exclamation points into coherent, understandable ... and hopefully meaningful – interesting reading!!! The cover really should say by Gary Ringger WITH Marla and Megan. And to Bill, Linda and Gail for fine-tuning our writings a bit more. Thanks Jaron for designing the cover and the page layouts.

- Most of all thanks to my heavenly Father and His Son, our Lord Jesus who planned and prospered my journey. (Jeremiah 29:11)

ENDNOTES

1. This is my title for a portion of a poem whose author is unkonwn. I found the full poem in Tim Hansel's book Holy Sweat (which I highly recommend) and there it was titled "The Road of Life".

2. Reader's Digest article. Does Prayer Heal? March 1996 Issue, pg 153.

3. Buford, Bob. Halftime. Zondervan, Grand Rapids, MI. 2008.

4. Swindoll, Charles R. The Mystery of God's Will. W Publishing Group, Division of Thomas Nelson, Inc. Nashville, TN 1999.

5. Burkett, Larry. Business by the Book. Thomas Nelson, Inc. Nashville, TN 1998.

6. Shirer, Priscilla. Gideon. Lifeway Press, Nashville, TN. pg 108.

7. Blackaby, Henry T. and King, Claude V. Experiencing God. Lifeway Press, Nashville, TN. 1990. Unit 1, pg 15.

8. Chambers, Oswald. My Utmost for His Highest. Dodd, Mead & Company, Inc. 1935.

9. You can listen to their story on this link: *www.radicalbusiness.co/resources*. It's a fun 17 minute video clip about how God uses ordinary people for extraordinary purposes when they commit their lives (and their businesses) fully to Him.